unfold

poetry + prose

ari b. cofer

**this collection comes with the following content warnings.
read at a gentle pace.**

familial + generational trauma, depression, anxiety, and ptsd
suicidal ideation + suicidal intent, self-harm, sexual assault
sex, drug + alcohol use + other tough topics

central
avenue
PUBLISHING

2023

Published by Central Avenue Publishing, an imprint of Central Avenue Marketing Ltd.
www.centralavenuepublishing.com

UNFOLD

Trade Paperback: 978-1-77168-284-8
Ebook: 978-1-77168-285-5

Published in Canada
Printed in United States of America

1. POETRY / African American & Black   2. POETRY / Women Authors

1 3 5 7 9 10 8 6 4 2

praise

"Ari's writing is breathtakingly brave in its vulnerability and ability to give words to things our hearts can't quite make sense of — this collection is no exception."

— Megan Jayne Crabbe, author of *Body Positive Power*, writer, and presenter

"*Unfold* is a collection filled with heartbreaking nostalgia, a home for grief. Ari B. Cofer does not hide from themselves in this collection. She crafts a universe without judgment and gives you a chance to look at all the parts of yourself, past and present, with honesty and acceptance."

— Michaela Angemeer, author of *you'll come back to yourself*

"Ari B. Cofer's beautifully heart-wrenching poems are an excavation of self, an exploratory journey through the muck of hardships that ultimately make us who we are. These poems are a guide through the trenches with the promise of a hard-won hope on the other side. *Unfold* is a gorgeous collection that digs deep and strikes gold."

— Sheleen McElhinney, author of *Every Little Vanishing*

author's note

i wanted to create a book of poetry + prose that successfully explored the ache
we feel when we begin to grow. but, like all works of art, it transformed into
its own entity, an honest tale about learning how to unfold ourselves to find
the place where we started.

this collection bloomed from the hardest year of self-discovery i have
endured. like many collections of poetry, not all pieces are historically
accurate, literal, or real, but every feeling described is undeniably me.

because it was therapeutic to write about the difficult questions, i named the
protagonist after myself—ari. my beginnings are similar to the ari in this
collection, but this separation from self was a healing experience. it allowed
me to write the version of myself i have always been striving towards and
interrogate the versions of myself i left behind.

these stories are mine, but they are also yours. they are your mother's and
father's and sister's and brother's. i hope this collection allows you to reflect
on your own unfolding, share a mirror with your inner child, and forgive the
person you are now.

we all come from somewhere, and we are all still growing into ourselves.
we will never stop. and wow,   what a beautiful, beautiful thing that is.

step 1
pick the defining moment

runaway

i don't go home,   because of the traffic.

because of the distance.

because i don't feel like declining the pyramid scheme recruitment
          parties hosted by my high school bully.

because i moved away and never moved on.

i don't go home,

because the new owners of our house painted the door blue.

because all of their roses are blooming and i'm still mourning my youth
buried underneath.

i don't go home,

because i'm afraid i'll run into my ex at braum's and i'll want him to kiss
          me while i'm waiting for my milkshake.

because i'll want to forget how it feels to be grown up.

because i'll pretend to be hot and heavy and seventeen again.

because chasing heartbreak hurts less than finding myself did.

i don't go home,

because i don't want to.

because i can't.

because it hasn't looked like home since i left.

because it feels even lonelier.

because i've made a new one.

because i don't ever, *ever* want to go back to where i used to be.

inner child

i rediscovered myself on a friday night.

we were watching a movie when
he slid his hand under my dress
and up my thigh,
       and then i was
in his car as he kissed my chest.
it's when i was naked that i remembered who i was before
there was any need to cover up. i was
a child and the world was
a meadow of becomings.   i could lie anywhere i wanted.

maturing brought a bruised neck
from a boy who didn't know how to hold
the ripening.
i wasn't warned i would be asked to bloom
in the back of a car
and left to masquerade
as the woman i was told i should be.

i have always been an almost,   aching
for growing pains,
locking my youth in the same drawer as the training bras.

i didn't know my girlhood would find her way
back to me.
that she would hold my budding hostage.

i kept her inside, and it makes sense that she came
when he did.

so, welcome home, inner child.
god, look at how much   *you've missed.*

roots

i hear the bones of our house relax into its foundation,
and i empathize with the ache of settling.
when i build a nest,
i can only rest long enough to fall in love
with the view,
before anyone can consider me
part of the landscape.

it's no wonder i've never had a chance
to unpack all this lonely.
when someone asks who i am,
there isn't enough time to search through the rubble.

i want to plant roots
because i know   growth tourniquets grief—

but home is the wind.
and it's only a matter of time
before i am pushed away
again.

etymology

don't run from who you are.
— *c. s. lewis,* prince caspian

grief was my becoming.
the doctors reached into the belly of a beacon
and ripped out a silhouette of her
yearning;

my mother surveyed me, bloodied and new,
and gave me the hebrew name for *lion.*
it was always my fate to live in the captivity of my mind.

in grade school,
i learned of aslan and how he freed the world,
and i'm just trying to hold it together
to protect my pride.

to be endangered is to know that you will never have
a gentle survival.
it's knowing you must always fight,
or prepare the world for the day
when all that remains
are stories about the way
you lived
and lived
and lived
until there was
nothing left
of you.

when you're older you'll understand

at four and a half years old i sang
over the grandfather clock
whose chimes chased the sun.
my mother bundled me in my grandmother's quilt
and said i was the best bedtime story there ever was.

a daughter who made gods out of
a soldier and a social worker.
a renegade who waited as long as she could
before running from what mattered.

i knew the passage of time would eventually
lead me to a reluctant becoming.

at twenty-five and a half years old
i am heavy and swollen from the burden
of another today. there is no relief
from pushing through.
it hurts and hurts and hurts,
and there is no until.

i hope i don't hear the clock stop singing
before i finally reach   myself.

i don't have enough time to feel this much

introductions

my name is **ari**, short for **arielle**, but not like the mermaid, because i'm
still finding my footing. i am known to stumble towards anyone looking
for anything. i make homes out of every heart that sees me.

my name is **ari** or **arielle** or **arielle britney**, and i hate the way my name
sounds in a stranger's mouth. every new introduction is a grade school
roll call. a tongue twister you try until you hate the sound of me.

my name is **ari**, but you knew that. my friends call me ari because they
love me, and
i think my father forgets to call me   because he doesn't.

my name is **ari, ari, ari,** and i am sick of having a name that rhymes with
an apology. my first cry was a curse. to break it would be to say *sorry for
the mess i've made by existing.*

i want you to know my name because it is all i have left of me.
it is all you will ever need to know.

6'3"

i'm five years old and my father is a giant.
he's big and loud, and my mom says it's because we are from a family of
fighters.
i don't know what this means, because
>   i'm known to run from any battle.

i'm five years old and my father is home again
and he does not know the way i like
>   *my sandwiches—crust on, diagonal cut.*   *ugh, mayo.*

giants are useless.
they take up space, and
they are mean when i want to go outside
and have something other than a father's presence
make me feel small.

i love my father.
maybe
it's because my mom tells bedtime stories where he's the hero.
a man in a faraway country who would return
with a suitcase of sympathy.

my dad came back with a porcelain vase.

>   at five years old, i was afraid that being a daughter
>   of a giant would mean i, too, would one day
>   be both up close and ten feet away
>   from the people   i loved,

and i didn't want to be like him:
out of reach but always revolving.
always adding space
to the emptiness that comes
with

distance.

somebody

i want a becoming
but i am not divine enough
for genesis.

my friends say i am already good.
i say *no*,
i am a bible in a motel nightstand.
brimming with stories of salvation.
            the least interesting thing in the room.
most days, i can barely catch my breath
as my lungs chase yearning.
turns out,
the true terror in revelation is not the rapture
of who i have prayed to be;
the terror is understanding the truth:

i'm not sure if i'll ever know who i am.

rap legend dmx dies at 50 and my father is 49

i can't process this, because it forces me to think about a day where i won't have my dad. *but that's already happened.* i know. but i don't think about that. i think of when i called him in the midst of wedding planning to say, "daddy, we have to dance to 'daughters' by john mayer" and he replied, "what if we dance to our song?" *will smith wrote "just the two of us" about the son he never talks about.* don't say that. i love my dad and he loves me. when his grandmother died, i found him in his office, achy and puffy-eyed. i held him, and i think part of me has never let go. *but when he found out you wanted to die, where was he? your mom picked you up from school crying, and he couldn't even leave work early to—* no. he was always there, even when he wasn't. after my first heartbreak, he knocked on my bedroom door and said he was there if i wanted to talk. *you never did.* i never wanted to. *why not?* because i couldn't. *because he was never the father you wanted him to be.* i am a daddy's girl. *you are your father's daughter.* I DON'T WANT HIM TO DIE YET. *some people lose their dad when they're young. yours didn't come home until kindergarten.* he has always loved me. *then why wasn't he there?* to support me and mom. *do you think he was anxious about bringing you into the world?* should i be okay knowing any day might be his last day in it? *no. but you must be okay admitting that your dad is not the legend you thought him to be. he taught you how to drive but could rarely guide you. he provided but rarely gave. yes, he loves you more than he's loved anything. it doesn't change the fact that you only talk to him on sundays. he may not be dead yet but god, was he ever really alive to you?* shut up. my dad is my dad, and he will always be the best one there was. and when he turns 50, i'm going to tell him i love him. and he will smile and kiss my cheek and tell me he loves me too.

i'll think about the rest when he's gone.

(desert)ion

a thousand mirages in the shape of
bodies approach me.
i know one is my mother and another is my father
because i recognize the parts of them
that look like me.
the rest are bodies of all the selves i have been.
i am a guest among my yesterdays,
holding hands with past loves,
with the drunk girl at the bar.
i am bloodstained and bruised
like a summer strawberry.
i can't handle the sight of my past anymore.

there is no optimism in survival,

only in forgetting.

veterans day

every november i call my father to say
fuck you for leaving me and
he hears *thank you for your service.*
he says *i love you, sweet daughter*
and i mute the phone to scream.

every november i try to forget to call my father
but the goddamn commercials remind me
all month long.
he's surprised i remembered and
i'm surprised he wants to keep talking.
i forget how to be a daughter when i hear his voice
so i joke about old age. time passing. nostalgia for the days we thought
we would have.

every november my father asks if i'm
seeing anyone new
and of course i say *no*
and my lie echoes through the bathroom
of the stranger i'm fucking.
i end the call and the stranger wants me
to come to bed
and call him *daddy.*
i do it because the word has never meant anything
to me anyway.

every november i call my father and say *hey dad*
and he says *hey baby, everything okay?*

and i say *yeah, just calling to say happy veterans day*
and he says *oh, okay, thanks, i love you*
and i say *i love you too*

and i do.
i promise, i do.

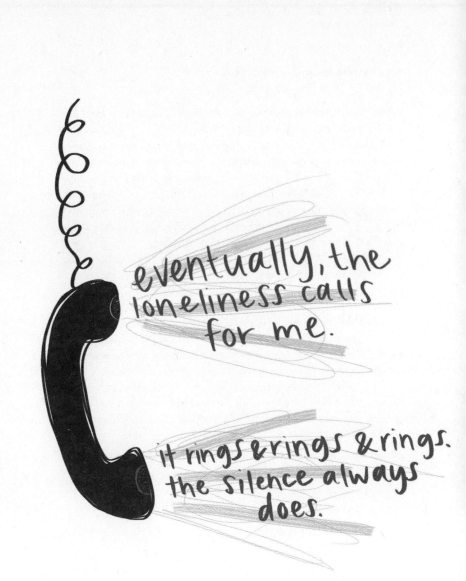

sunday phone call, reimagined

hey mom, do you ever get random aches in your knees? how long does it last? only when it's cold? arthritis? *hereditary?*   mom, i was kinda dizzy when i woke up this morning, and gerald says that happens sometimes when people have anemia. do we have low iron? should i get checked? what do i ask?   mom, this is my fourth uti this year and i don't know what i'm doing wrong.   mom, i think i'm doing everything wrong.   mom, have i ever done anything right?   mom, if my only accomplishment is healing the body you made for me, that's not a life worth celebrating.
mom, i'm sorry.   mom, i need you.   mom, when you were still my home, did you feel full or just swollen?   mom, you know i'm a poet. i'm just trying to ask if you wanted me.
mom, did you want me?   mom, when i was sixteen, you admitted you used to wish your daughter would be your best friend.
        mom, if i can remember how to be a daughter, is it too late to be your friend?   mom, my head hurts.
mom, everything hurts and you're the only person i ever want to tell.
        mom, what happened to me?   mom, *something* happened and now i don't want you around but i still need you close.
        mom, why does it hurt to want you?   mom, are you listening, what happened?

why can i only remember the good times when the home videos are on?

why can't i let you in when i don't even remember pushing you out?
mom, what happened?   mom, why am i like this?

did you pass this down to me?

did your mother pass it to you?   mom, do you know when it ends?   mom, has it ever ended?

hey mom, do you remember that picture of me after i cut off all my hair?

when you said *you're starting to look less like your father and more like me.*
        mom, i am trying to look for myself and keep finding you.

do you have any time to talk?

a written complaint to my parents, god, or the universe

zero out of ten execution.
highly dissatisfied with quality of existence.
your job was to bring the sun and create beauty,
and i feel like i'm only living to justify the end.
tell me, mom, dad, god, universe,
how do i begin to want this if i know it can never truly be mine?
if it can be over in the blink of an eye, why even look to begin with?
mom, dad, god, universe,
i'm so fucking angry because you've made someone
who wants to thank you for the gift of breath,
but i think it was just because you didn't want it for yourself.
god, you spent seven days creating the birds and the oceans,
and we have never gotten out of that goddamn flood.
universe, when is the next big bang, or has all that will happen already
finished?
will i be like the stars, dead and still chasing everything ahead of me?

you are who you are until you leave them behind

there is no safe place in this world for a preteen. at twelve years old, the galaxy is just a jealous sky. holding every almost. keeping it a wish away.

at twelve, my budding heart couldn't understand the process of uprooting. i was on AIM when my parents announced our move across state lines. i refused to believe how much could change in an instant.

everything is apocalyptic when you're twelve, even when it really is. my friends promised they'd still love me even when i left. this was a falsehood i'm still unlearning.

by now i know that most times, people only love when it's easy. people leave and never come back, and forgetting is easier than wanting. this was not a good cocktail for a girl with a lightweight heart. my birth was the big bang. in the beginning, there were two college students in love. a graduation. a shotgun wedding. and me. these days, my therapist says that sometimes i want to die because i feel like i was never supposed to be here. i tell her that sometimes i want to die because i never asked to be.

there are notebooks at my parents' house buried under the remnants of my youth. they are full of scribbles and gel-pen hearts that narrate this part of my life:

> *i hate this so much*
> *i don't want to do this*
> *they can't make me*
> *i hate everything*
> ~~*i want to stop breathing*~~

so this is how it starts. doctors say dormant mental illness is often triggered by a life-changing event. i wonder how my sadness didn't wake sooner. when my father was deployed. when my sister was sick. when the girls would tug at my twists and say *your hair is so gross. it looks like a spider. it would be better straight. you would be better whit—*

now, the only memories i have of my youth are the ones i stuffed into corners.

on my first day in the new school, i bit my cheeks as i walked down the hallways. waited for my eyes to drown the whole place. the cool girls parted the crowds. they were all white. all blonde. all wearing hollister and abercrombie. that night, i swore to my journal that i would never shop at jcpenney again. everything is a stereotype inside the walls of a middle school. i went to the wrong class. forgot my locker combination. sat alone at the lunch table until i found a friend willing to adopt a stray. middle school will chew up your adolescence and spit out a stranger. i have never wanted more to be wanted.

so i changed. it's hard for me to know who i was before all of this. i molded myself into a pretender. now, every other version of myself feels fake.

the coming-of-age story always ends with a cliché. i found friends who loved me as i continued to fall out of love with myself. we torpedoed through the halls and mimicked our science teacher. belted linkin park and slipknot and taylor swift on the bus ride home. passed notes in class about how crushing a crush could be. said *i love you* because we did. we really, truly did.

when i moved out of my parents' house, i found my history notebook decorated with stickers and sharpie-d with my name in the seasick cursive of a twelve-year-old. inside the cover, i found that i had written one phrase over and over and over and over:

let me die.

as a preteen, i think i thought it was poetry. today, i know it might as well have been my first suicide note. in my teenage bedroom, i could not find the parts of myself i left behind when i tried to become the person everyone wanted. i learned to hate birthdays and jump ropes and the way the sky looked when there was only me and the darkness. both hungry for life and starving for someone else's love.

each day i wonder who i could've been if i were the one to love myself
        back.

life is so hard, tommy. sometimes i think it's the hardest thing there is.

—chuckie finster, rugrats

i am four and standing in the kitchen / the metronome thuds / of my father chopping strawberries with a knife that echoes / in a hollow apartment / as if to say *arielle, arielle, arielle* / *do you hear me* / i see him but i am listening to the television / because it is the morning / and there are only wonderful things / in the morning / *arielle, arielle, arielle* / and the xylophone sings through the television / and i yell with joy / because it is the morning / and a new episode of *rugrats* always plays in the morning / so i run / *arielle* / to the living room beyond the moon-high laminate countertops / *arielle* / i catch on the rug / *ARIELLE* / spill into the coffee table / a knife falls to the tile / the metronome becomes footsteps becomes cries / my mouth is another sliced fruit / i am upset / because this is not how mornings should go / it is not wonderful to run towards happiness and be left spitting up blood / *it is not wonderful to remember this* / when i was four i was in the kitchen / and i think it was my mother but / i wanted it to be my father / who watched my first suicide attempt / except i wasn't trying to die / back then / but they would never learn the difference / all they ever see / in me / is a star collapsing / my fire will scorch no matter how far i run / that day i knew / i would always hold them back with the gravity / of my presence / i am not the only one who loves / out of routine / i don't remember cleaning the blood / but i know it was only a matter of time / before i ran from the call of my name / into wanting / i was born to a soldier and a therapist / it is in my veins to surrender to emotion / now, i am older / and learning that if someone cares for me / they will beg for my love / my forgiveness / until their siren song lures me in / until their heart clogs my throat / until i am left with a mouthful / of blood / to remember / the parts *that hurt* / *the most*

25

step 2
name a beloved

we were happy

you kissed me in the shower | made me sunday breakfast | **loved me** *|*
harmonized with me in the car | warmed my feet with your thighs | **loved**
me *| said you wanted forever | asked to be my muse |* **loved me | loved me**
| loved me—

but we insulted each other across the target parking lot after i cried the
whole ride there
and pierced each other with our jagged edges
and felt uncomfortable in the discomfort,
so we exhausted each other
and grieved what was left
and i really, truly hate
that you made
the right decision
to leave.

I HATE YOU FOR
ABANDONING
THE PARTS OF ME
THAT YOU DIDN'T
WANT TO LOVE

a spiral of forevers

i have fallen in love four times
and have never been able to pull out of it.
i was stuck
reaching for those who could catch a spark
on my beating heart.
when it went out, i would
      STRIKE and STRIKE and STRIKE
until i burned the memory down.
i can't hold a beginning
without smothering it.

so i'll sacrifice my sun and my sky and my breath
to keep the flame
going.

cozy, warm, treacherous

he's comfortable.
a free fall, a good nap, a resolved melody.
i sank into his eyes the day we met,
and i was delicate and pruned and small
when i finally came up for air.

it's normal for love to feel like this.
a smooth whiskey—
painless until you've had too much of it.

he's there when i double over from the burn of an empty-bottle promise.
he promises to change and loves me harder and pours me another glass.

i keep taking what he gives because
he's comfortable.
he's my home.

and i've always been such a homebody.

fujita scale

nine years ago, you called me from your storm
shelter when the tornado
sirens went off. *please come over. i don't want to be*

alone. the weather radio teased
the worst-case scenarios. the wind threatened me,
branches thrown at my windows.

the entire sky had to fall
before you needed me.

the curse of vulnerability

i love at a distance.
let them get too close and they'll have scars from when i'm forced to let
go.

one friday in may, i decided to be in love with cole.
i walked behind him across the center stage, high school diploma in
hand, adulthood waiting for me on the steps down.
    "we did it," he said, and we kissed
in the parking lot and at his mother's house and all over oklahoma city.
    "and together we'll go to the ends of the earth."

when i ran towards the edge, he pulled me home by the wrist, bloody and
hungry and scared for the end.
    "you did this to yourself?"
    "i don't know how else to let this out."
    "are there more?"
i pulled up my shorts to reveal a battlefield.
    "you don't have to be alone on the front line."
    "but i want to be."

we were sitting on the curb by his house, letting the ache fade with the
daylight. the darker it became, the more he understood. the more he
promised a healing love. the moon and the streetlamps haloed his face,
and then, the paramour angel kissed me.

i unfolded, thawed, felt the burden of exposure.
i was seen, and it hurt.
i was see-through, blanketing the sidewalk, ready for the sun.

cole left me two weeks later. i am sobering up and dry heaving the memories from the withdrawals. he's still under my fingernails, and i wonder if he tells the story of how he got his scars. i wonder if i will ever learn my lesson, stop digging into beating hearts like it will be my last supper, and reach out, bare all that i have left, and embrace the bending that leads to growth.

proverbs 31

i was eight years old, under the timeless cherry-colored stained-glass windows of my grandmother's church. *stand up*, she said, *it's time to worship.* i stood and sang the prayers with a sore tongue.

the pastor raised his hands to say *the woman is the neck and the man is the head.* i didn't understand, but i said *amen* anyway.

maybe it's because god is man. he created girl, and girl is only good when she agrees. he knows a girl could praise any man who showed her love. he knows i am not a girl who could back down from her father.

i am eighteen when a boy says i am a gift delivered from angels. says i am good because i am mild. because i am not easy. he wants to get closer,closer,closer, and i let my nerves drain out of my veins and stain the bedsheets.

maybe god will let me resist if he sees there's nothing left inside to take. when i want to say *no*, i close my eyes and pretend i'm in the library, lying between the aisles of religious texts and poetry. some days i don't see much of a difference between them. the library is empty, and i scream the word *NO* until the echoes bring me back

to his breath. there is no safe space for a girl who was never taught to be honest. who was taught to say *yes* when really, she would pray to run loudly from the shadows of womanhood.

I DON'T KNOW WHY I'M STILL HERE.
IT'S OKAY TO NOT KNOW. BUT I'M SO GLAD YOU ARE.

how it began, how it must always be

he buys me a drink and we say *bottoms up*. we are wild and young
and all-knowing, and i forget his name between the cider and the old-
fashioned. *be good for me*, he says, and i am already
writing the poem in my head.
             HOW TO LOSE YOURSELF:
             A MANUAL OF BECOMING.
i don't *want* to listen to him, but i do. i am warm and blurry and love to
be noticed.
to be wanted is magical
even when it's fake. i don't want to be his, but i am,
and i think that's womanhood. we are most girl when we ignore the ache,
and i am drunk and numb and ambling to his bed. we are most girl
when we're kidnapped by the hands of time
after falling into the arms of a wandering man—
                         this is how it began and how it must always be.

i give myself to a man who swears to hold me. i lose myself in a
stumbling, toxic love,
and all i do is   endure.

disillusioned

did i romanticize this?

because being loved by you was a quiet revolution.
i fell to my knees and surrendered to your 11 p.m. call.
i'll keep coming if you ask me to.
a fairy tale has a lover and a villain,
but is it still enchanting if they become the same person?

to admit that i love you is a half-truth.
we could promise to love each other
for all of ever after,
but i really don't think we could
call it happily.

i am the fool in this story.
believing you'd rescue me
from the grips of the shadows,
but instead you held me captive
in the memories.

i still tell our love story to everyone.
the legend of the girl who lived and loved you,
even when the fantasy didn't want me back.

you're mine, best friend, all mine

i loved him wrong.
we blamed teenage lust and jose cuervo
and everything except our colliding hands,
our revving breaths,
our barricades crashing into the sheets.

we didn't make love;
we made a mess out of it.
the morning sun flared onto the wreckage:
a totaled friendship, an aching whiplash.
he joked about baby names and co-parenting and vasectomies,
i thanked him for the coffee and plan b.

we said i love you, goodbye.
he called;   i didn't answer.
he stopped trying;   i missed my friend.
i wanted to hold his hand and sleep in his bed—
not to be drunk and hot and raging.
to be sixteen again. blowing through red lights,
smoking out of an apple bong.
lying beside each other under the moonlight and calling every star the
way home.

                wishing for a friendship that lasts.

                loving them right, if it does.

virtue

it's cold in october but katie, she leaves her living room windows open anyway. hunter and andrew and laurie are also there, rolling their eyes at the sex scene in the movie we're watching. it's clear i'm the only virgin here, and i don't hide it. anyone with a heart still intact doesn't lie about the things they've lost.

to my friends, i am the warm room, the belly laugh. to my mother, i am enough, maybe. to hunter, the boy tangled and cuddled by me in katie's cold living room, i am a body. i think he maybe loves me, and i love anyone who wants any part of me. i am wrapped in a blanket and his hand is on the inside of my leg and he asks if i want to leave. *what am i if not evanescent?*

we run out the front door and suddenly i am tongue-tied under the magnolia tree. we kiss and feel and toy. when he asks if i want to leave with him, i nod. i would give anything to anyone who asked for it.

we follow the breeze to his car, careful not to wake the neighborhood, the weight of our youth crushing the leaves beneath us. we climb inside and park in an empty lot. the moon lights the car, and our breath masks the rest.

it's always cold in october, and i know this because all of my layers end up on the floor of his chevy.

he doesn't say thank you but says he'll drive me home.
i button my jeans, but it feels like he's still inside me and i am not.
i wonder if this is what sex is,
collecting bodies to use them as armor.
we can't see grief under our bed
if we're on someone else's mattress.

i cry in the shower because
loving myself makes me feel
more naked than intimacy ever could.
because fucking an empty vessel is easier than admitting
i am becoming one.

april fools'

the joke wasn't the way you loved me,
it was the way you left.

here i am,
puffy and bloated from believing all your tricks.
where did you want me? under your table saw? locked out of sight?
drowning in the tank
      with the sharks
           and the stingrays
                as i *BANG, BANG, BANGED*
on the glass—

our love was never a stunt,
because i still feel all of it.
i hope one day i'll forget how i loved myself more
when you called me baby.
i wish the love was fake.
i would let you leave me over and over again
if your palms weren't bloodstained from my tenderness.

i can't believe another april has come
and you are still just a disappearing act.

the first time, as it happened, completely

i was barely eighteen and hated waking up alone, or at all.

most mornings, my roommate made her breakfast and tore the curtains wide open as if to devour the sun. some still wonder if i am the reason she never could. rays peeked through the unwashed windows and made the dusty air look like glitter. i liked to pretend i was a snow globe's protagonist, my dorm the glass dome. this way, my world was still beautiful even if it flipped upside down.

my routine never changed, because i never did. no eighteen-year-old ever does. we're invincible, smoking marlboros on abandoned rooftops. moaning about the pain of becoming. how we'll never go home, even when the moon comes.

the day was two months before my suicide attempt, and there was no self-harm like suffocating under someone else's weight. the name isn't important. he was almost thirty and living with his mom and said i was the most beautiful girl he'd ever seen.

there are a lot of days i wish i'd tried to kill myself sooner.

when night fell and the curtains closed, i snuck to my date with a man who picked me like a dandelion. when he saw me walk outside, he honked twice and waved once. he had the same type of car that cops drove. i still check for him in my rearview.

the car smelled fake-new.
a magician masking the truth.

"you're even cuter in person," he said.

i snuck a glance at my knight in shining dodge charger. he looked like

45

every other frat boy i'd fucked. brotherhood isn't really fellowship, it's unfamiliarity with the way their sisters cry about the men who look like them. i buckled in and he drove us to the 7-eleven down the road.

"a gas station?" i asked.
"trust me," he said. "they have the best vanilla lattes, and i'm getting you one."

he left me idle with the car, intentions in motion.
he returned with two drinks.

"cheers," i said.
"i figured we'd be up for a while." he smiled. "can i have a kiss for that?"
"for getting me coffee?"
"c'mon, please? i've been wanting to kiss that pretty face of yours since i saw it pop up on my screen."
"i'm not convinced," i replied.
"i'll convince you." he traced his fingers across my thigh until they made a home beneath the fabric of my dress. the pressure felt ten thousand pounds. there's no forgiving a heavy hand.

i hesitated. i kissed him. i was supposed to.

he drove me back to campus and walked me through the streets he took as a former student. today, a memory lane that hurts to go down.

"i love girls like you," he said.

i think i responded, but there are a lot of things i think i did. he was gripping my hand in his as we walked along the sidewalk. i think i tried to pull away, but maybe i didn't. he led me to a bench on the outskirts of the university. he asked to put his arm around my shoulders and i didn't answer, and he did it anyway. we didn't say anything for a while, and

his hand drifted from my shoulder to my arm to my shoulder to my neck. i thought i'd felt the worst there was, but the ache always returns. this is a world with no bottom. we fall until the wind chooses to stop holding us back.

and i was on that bench next to that man. he traced my jawline and tilted my face towards his. i try not to believe this accident was my fault, but the truth is that i didn't swerve enough. i should've seen it coming. he kissed me. i heard my heart screeching and the sound of his breath and the cicadas singing my grave song around us.

"i didn't expect to like you this much."
"we don't really know each other."
"that's what's so amazing about it, huh?"

he stood and stretched. sometimes i forget how big a man can be.

"wanna go back to my place?"

i shook my head.

"not tonight."
"that's okay," he said after a beat. "i'll take you home."

we walked from the bench to the car and let the sound of the engine fill the silence.

i thought about how every movie has that moment. the one right before the ultimate resolution, the protagonist's "all is lost" moment. where they're vulnerable, lost, helpless, scared.

this is where i found myself. searching for hope inside a car with a man who picked up a teenager from her dorm.

"can i ask why?" he was soft.
"why what?" the blinker switched on and matched my heart's tempo.
"well, i thought the vibes were good, and you'd come over . . ."

he pulled into traffic,

and i felt bad. his eyes were soft and he was kind. i was just anxious. reading into it too much. sure, he touched me and kissed me, and it wasn't what i wanted. but it's okay. how else would i know i was wanted?

"i'm just nervous, i guess."
"to have sex?"
"yeah," i lied.
"are you a virgin?"
"yeah," i lied.
"oh," he said. "i wouldn't have guessed."

i didn't respond, and he pulled into a gravel parking lot behind the local crossfit. there was one streetlight, me, him, and the entire night sky.

all was lost.   and i was alone.

he turned off his headlights and reached across the middle console and grabbed my face. he kissed me and i couldn't breathe. i pulled away to say

"i thought you were taking me—"

he interrupted with another kiss.

"take me home," i said with my eyes open.

he grabbed my waist and pulled me over the center console until i was straddling his lap. i wanted to fight but i was trying not to cry. he kissed from my collarbone to my neck to my ear. i get sick when people play with their food.

"i am going to show you what sex feels like," he whispered.

i have decided not to detail what happened after.
time healed the wound,
but the scar is still so
fucking
big.

when he was done, i dissociated in the passenger seat as he laughed about how turned on i must have been. he dropped me at my dorm, and i washed the blood out of my underwear in the community bathroom sink.

i was home but it was still happening. the worst parts replayed and replayed, and i would have done anything to stop watching. i closed the curtains before going to sleep.

i want to move past this nightmare,
but i'm too scared to go through.

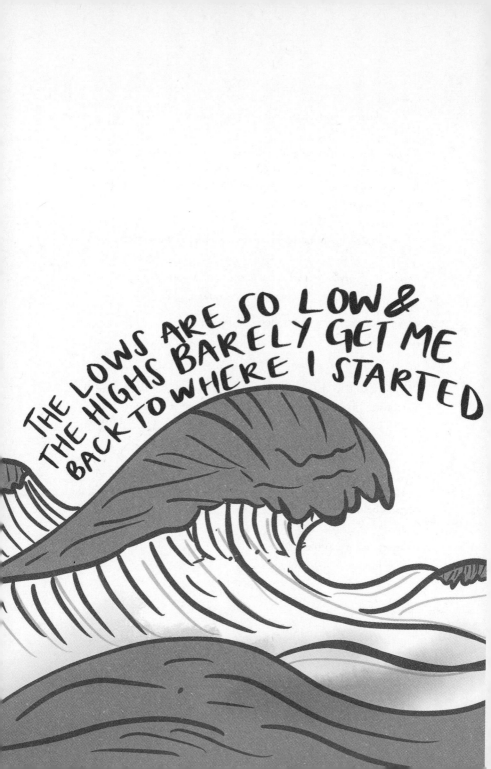

domestic

i remember settling into our mess.
my walls crumbled, and you said you loved
a fixer-upper.   i wanted to be fixed
because i wanted to be yours.
the carpet was tear-stained and covered with a hand-me-down rug,
the doors were stubborn and i could never close them behind me.
we watched reruns of *ink wars* until you ran your hand up my thigh and
i remembered
i was someone else's. i remembered how it hurts
to make a mess out of womanhood. moaning
this feels so good until it drowns out the hum of the heater.
believing it, really trying hard to believe
that i loved you, and not the roof or the doors, or anything else that felt
safe.

so, did we ever build something worth growing into?
is this where your heart really is?

life is a scary movie that i can't turn off

fade in.

LOST GIRL shuffles into a house party to find herself at the bottom of
    the trash can punch.

LOST GIRL's thoughts are drowned by the music, her anxiety's lullaby.

LOST GIRL sits. sees drunk bodies stumble over their secrets and
    solo cups.

LOST GIRL drinks until the butterflies drown.

LOST GIRL relaxes and sings and attracts a LOST BOY.

LOST GIRL loses herself in the harmony until she remembers the first
    time she heard this song.

LOST GIRL hears the LOST BOY rewrite the lyrics.

LOST GIRL shoves the grief into her stomach.

LOST GIRL prays the butterflies will still be kind after all of this.

LOST GIRL waits for it all to end.

fade out.

are you lying to yourself?

yes.

i mean, no.
i mean, maybe.
i mean, is it *really* lying to myself if i say i wanted it? that he loved
me?

when he tells me i am good when i am quiet, i resist
the impulse to cry under his body.
i definitely wanted it because he said
i was the prettiest at the party.
i kissed him first and he pushed
too far.

it turns out, even monsters feel desire.
i only wanted to be needed.

**the commonalities between the girl flirting with me on pike
street and me seeing my ex-boyfriend in the target parking lot**

i wasn't prepared for this.

i stop to talk because they want me to. because i've had this daydream
and i *really* need a happy ending. *yes, i stall*—i want this moment to feel
so full that i struggle to carry the memory home. i am fluttery and warm
and earnest because i love someone the hardest when it's all pretend.
when *i know i'm not supposed to.*

i say i'm glad i ran into them,
and they say i'm the most beautiful thing
that's happened to them today.
and then,
like always,

      they leave.

a heart breaks louder than a tree falls

in other words, i suffered in complete silence. i kissed men who kissed the
fantasy of me. cradled myself on someone else's mattress. said,

maybe, i don't know,

when i meant

not again.

i was a corpse, the way i would lie. honesty was loud and the noisy truth
was oblivion. i wanted a quiet death so i called it euthanasia. if i can't stop
the fall, why bother making a noise?

i tried anyway.

it wasn't enough. he knew the echo of a heartbreak. the grief bounced
back on him and filled the room, and he called me a rough girl. a good
and loud and giving girl. i fell into his bed when he had me all alone.
would you believe me if i said i

couldn't, wouldn't, didn't

make a single fucking sound?

should i put "emo" in my dating bio?

his hands slowed when he reached
where my thigh meets my hip, and joked that it felt like braille.
i asked him not to   read into it.

i am used to this.
i have been sixteen, modeling a sweatshirt in my bedroom on an august
afternoon.
my first cocktail tasted of blood and neosporin.
rusty gillettes in phone cases.
30% off bracelets from claire's.
stolen pencil sharpeners.

i've made this bed of scars, so i can't complain
when the gauze duvet becomes uncomfortable.
when i suffocate by stuffing myself inside nightstand drawers.

what you keep hidden eventually makes a home inside your chest.
the secrets will spill into the corners and stain the tile.

i know how to clean a mess,
how to dodge the stares, and how to admit:

> *i don't want anyone to notice me fading.*

2012

i don't want to relive that day,
i just want to exist in the morning after,
when i saw the picture your mother sent me.

look, she said, and i did.
and it was us.
i wore a red dress, surrounded by a sea of somebodies.
you were steps away and buried within them.
we were looking at each other,
smiling as if we'd found the first dandelion of the summer.
i think we wished for each other too.

here i am, talking about the moment again.
i don't mean to do that. i just want to think about the picture.
i look closer, and you can see jenna's face. she's talking to erika about
the—
no, sorry, not the memory,
jenna is talking to erika.
there are so many faces, i couldn't count them if i tried.
i've never had a good memory.
anyway,

i can't believe you loved me, and i loved you,
and instead of loving each other we suffocated inside the almosts.
we drowned our heartbeats in the murmur of the crowd.

i don't even remember this happening.
the picture, that is.

not that moment.
well,
i guess that moment. everything is about this moment.
everything is about how my love for you was a photo album full of the
days you were good to me. and all of it was good. and still, i missed this
shot.
and still, i miss the memories.

on smallness

i shrank to fit his desire.
some days, i became the shape of a girl
who knew every player on the new england patriots.
other days, i was a stripped mannequin in his bed.
that's how he liked me, and that was fine. i would do anything
to dial him into my heart. i wanted him to listen to my heartbeat
and know that i would change the rhythm to whatever song he wanted
to hear.
i wanted to be another thing he couldn't get out of his head.
to love a boy like him was to perform the most sacred ritual.
the sacrificial girl always drowns in the linen sheets.
the prophetic boy becomes a god.

evolution, composed

one day i am sitting at a piano,
kissing a boy on the bench after playing
"chopsticks."
the next day, the boy takes me into his bedroom
and asks me to play him a whole symphony.

it shouldn't have happened, but it did.
we are mammals with god complexes and
it's human nature to submit to desire.
to the pull of his hands on my waist, my throat, my hair—

this is what it takes to evolve:
leaving behind the innocence,
chasing after passion,
ignoring the tidings,
and finally facing
the music.

step 3
choose what to heal

nearly, very nearly

i don't love me as much as i love what could've been,
                but i am trying to love me the most
                and forget about how i let go of hope
for oblivion.

resurrection

i'm better now, can't you *see?* my cheeks are dry and my chest is open,
because *look*—

every part of me is spilling over the pews, and the masses call this a
baptism.

if i talk about what hurts, it will have no power over me,

so i am baring it all in this confession. recovery is only a hail mary,

and i will do whatever it takes for you to believe me when i say,

i'm better, i'm better, i'm so fucking glad i'm alive because *look*—

my teeth. they're sharp and cracked from eating away at the torment until
i got my fill.

see? i'm not hollow anymore. i can't feel the sadness growing, except when

i do. it creeps up my throat and i try to swallow it down and i choke.
don't ask if i'm okay.

yes, i'm great. sometimes, the reminders of who i could have been   if i
wasn't who i became

sit in my stomach, and i carry them around until it burns.

the meds bring relief but i don't want to need them. i want to stretch my
pores and drain

this illness out of me.

say my prayers and hope it won't come back.   *i know* it will
because god is just as fucked-up as i am.

but don't   worry about me. i swear, i can save my soul. i'll bless my
body and my blood and call it eucharist.

i'll run from the darkness by swimming as deep into myself as i can. i'll
fantasize about which sin it would take to drown. i'll hold my breath
until the feeling passes. i'll come up for air and won't know why. i'll make
myself new, and you'll ask if i still feel the grief stirring inside of me. and
i'll say, no, not anymore. look at me.   i started over.

we are denying your appeal for additional treatment

have you tried yoga?

yes. i have. i would bend over backwards each day if it meant i wouldn't see the demons in front of me. i am not flexible enough to reach for the light anymore. after too much trauma, the body doesn't move the same. every inch of me is tearing as i try to unfold. i am trying, really trying, but none of it is working.

have you tried medication?

yes. i have. i chase effexor each day with my cold brew. i have been taking meds for so long that if you reach for me in the dark, you might mistake me for a bottle of lithium. there is no amount of refills that could satiate this emptiness. i am one skipped dose away from a casket. nothing i've tried can stop the wanting. the crumbling. the falling. the—

have you tried therapy?

YES. I HAVE. I WAS TOLD THE ONLY WAY TO HEAL IS TO OPEN UP. BUT LOOK AT ME NOW. I AM A THANKSGIVING TURKEY. ALL CARVED UP AND SPILLING OVER. THE WORLD IS HUNGRY AND MY LIMBS ARE TIED WITH A NOOSE. I CAN'T KEEP RUNNING AWAY FROM THIS. I AM HERE AND I DON'T WANT TO BE. ARE YOU LISTENING? I CAN'T KEEP SPLITTING MY CHEST OPEN JUST BECAUSE YOU DON'T BELIEVE ME WHEN I SAY MY HEART ISN'T BEATING. I HAVE TO RESUSCITATE MYSELF EVERY MORNING WITH A BOILING SHOWER. SOME DAYS I CAN'T EVEN DO THAT. TO KEEP LIVING IS TO BITE OFF MORE THAN I CAN CHEW. CAN YOU HEAR ME CHOKING? DO YOU WANT ME TO—

well, something is bound to work eventually.
it's not hard to pull yourself out of this.
just be a little stronger.

there's nothing more we can do for you.

trying

on the best day of my life, i wore a coffee-colored ballgown to hear my husband say *i'm so glad you're mine.* and so was i. love became a mouthful of wedding cake and aching feet; an echo of slow songs and clinking champagne glasses. we were too tired to have sex. we lay in bed and laughed at our palms, strawberry from running through the hotel lobby with suitcases full of the lives we used to have.

at the start of our love story, i reached into my throat and said, *here. have my voice. i've never known how to use it, anyway.* but he didn't want me quiet; he wanted to hear my groggy good-mornings and my pleas to kill the living room spiders and my harmonies to the grocery store radio.

but when we were angry, there was no foundation. we'd float around each other's chests and try to build homes inside the empty cavities. we'd whisper *i love you* in one ear and *goodbye* into the other. he'd lie and sneak and take and twist, and i'd let him hurt me however he wanted in the name of forever. he'd swear *i love you* but say he *can't fucking do this anymore.* i was bad at making him want me but so good at disappearing. i'd swallow pills and drive home, high at his call. i still don't know who i was trying to hurt more. i'd walk through the door and he'd see my body and say *where are you?* and i'd say *right in front of you, baby.* we'd fuck, because that's what angry lovers do. we'd cry after, because of course we would. we'd recall the better days to fill the space   between us. we'd get help because even when it all came crashing down, we still reached for each other from under the rubble.

i'd do anything for love, but i can't die for it. that would be the easy thing to do. when the sadness returns, i want something to let me leave, but his love doesn't ever let go. and for his love, i feed the dog and the cat in the morning so he can sleep in. i give him the drugs and the knives and say *please let this be the only thing you ever hide from me.*

our love is as effortless as it is backbreaking. our love works because we do not pretend it is easy. our love is good because we are fierce and loud and messy and we fight to keep it.

our love is worth speeding down I-35, windows down, screaming our wedding song to the wind. my love is something worth unfolding, worth staying, worth breaking,

worth living for.

a collection of sad, fucked-up thoughts i would never willingly admit to my friends

the group chat sends an old picture of me, squinty-eyed, laughing, loud,
and i delete it instead of responding.
your happiness is the most beautiful thing,
they say, and i sit on my hands to keep from sending
DON'T YOU SEE IT'S ALL FAKE.
i don't want to push them away so i push my heavy heart into my
stomach
and let the swallowed cries harden it.
i love you all so much, i send, and it's true.
i am warmest when i am building a memory with them, yelling sweet
nothings through times square,
crying on facetime. *we love you too,* they send,
and i wonder how much it would hurt them if it were the last time they
could.
i look through every photo we've ever sent each other and relive
the late-night poetry readings and couch cuddles and goodbye hugs. they
hold me tighter
than i've ever held myself, and now i'm crying because i don't want to be
another thing that is painful to remember. i want to steal their phones
and their brains and take away any part of me that still lives.
i want to sneak away, wide-eyed, resolved, quiet,
delete the chat,
stop pretending,
and disappear, just like so many other things we've loved
and swore would be here forever.

let's play a drinking game

if you say it out loud, you have to mean it.

if you're lying, **drink**.

i'm pretty good at this game;

i can convince anyone of almost anything. **drink**.

okay, fine, that was a practice round. i'll go again.

jake, i still think you're cute.

marie, i think you're cute too but i could never kiss a girl. **drink**.

okay, you caught me. should i keep going?

well, it's embarrassing, but i still jump over the sidewalk cracks to make sure my mother gets home safe. when i'm with people i love, i avoid eye contact on purpose to train them to forget me.

wow, wait, let me drink. that got sad.

the texture of sunny-side up eggs is a criminal offense.

love is just another thing that ends. **drink**.

okay, love is just another thing that starts shiny until it's just another penny on the street.

i'm afraid to swallow gum or watermelon seeds, because i'm afraid they'll take over and i'll die. **drink**.

okay, i'm afraid to give anything the chance to take root in me.

i'm not afraid of the dying part. **drink**.

no, i promise, that one is true! **drink**.

wow, do you want the truth? fine, i'm drunk, i'll say it—all of this scares me. i'm not afraid of the watermelon making a garden out of me, i'm just terrified of being a home. i'm not even my own. why else would i be here, coating my throat with tito's if not to douse the walls with gasoline. if not to wait for one of these truths to burn the whole fucking place down. god. i'm sorry. what was i talking about? fuck, that's right, sidewalks, my mother. speaking of her, my father texted me yesterday to say he loves me, and i believe him this time. **drink**.

i still love my father.

i need a refill.

god this is so fun! **drink**.

all of you here, i love you more than i love myself. i don't want to go home. i don't want to go home. what? no! i'm okay! **drink**.

this is just a game. **drink**.

that was the point of this. i needed to say it. i needed someone to hear it and i needed everyone to be drunk to not remember it. I WANT YOU TO FORGET ME. **drink**.

okay, i don't want you to forget me, but i'm going to leave anyway.

i'll be safe on the way home. **drink**.

the game is over.

the rules of honesty are conditional. we care only when it really matters.

i have to go. i'll see you tomorrow. let me finish my drink.

my ride is here.

tell me where it hurts.

i think it'd be easier to tell you where it doesn't.
making the choice to keep living is swallowing a live grenade with my
morning coffee.
the only way i am safe is if i keep the carnage inside.

does anyone know?

i don't want anyone to see the way i crumble.
someone will try to hold my hand,
but i refuse to let go of the trigger and let them.

what do you want to do?

the hardest part of living is knowing
how hard it is to forget,

and how easy it all can end.

TO KEEP
LIVING IS THE
MOST PAINFUL ACT
IN THE WORLD
&
THE BRAVEST THING
I HAVE EVER DONE.

affirmations

i love my body—   *no i don't.*
i've never been tender enough to love anything that holds me.
the moments in which i self-destruct are the only times
i have ever felt like i've done something worth remembering.
i picture the headlines:
PERSON TRAINS HEART TO STOP BEATING.
my thoughts are the most violent psalm, and they do not need a melody
to sing with.

i think i'm healing—   *no i don't.*
i haven't tried to hurt myself in a while, and it's somehow the most
painful thing i've ever done.
i am desperate to remember my skin before it was mine.
i think i was better off before i was me.

i want to say i love myself. but   *i don't.*
and i do.
i touch my skin and i am touching the universe.
my body fights for my life even when i don't,
and is that not the definition of a god?
i must be an atheist because i've never been able to believe in myself.
i've been on my knees, praying for a revelation.

i am trying to live and live and live until i can love myself without
second-guessing.
i am trying to live and live and live until i can finally love this body that
holds me.

i told my husband i didn't want kids, and i cried at his vasectomy

my favorite picture of my mother
is the one in which she is a bikini model
in the apartment she shared
with my father,
who needed to duck
to avoid hitting his head on the doorframes.
more obvious than her halle berry masquerade
is the way in which she carries me,
a burgeoning garden
still ripening in her
swollen belly.
she is barely twenty-three,
and smiling at my father just because he asks.

i think of the fading polaroid that is expectancy
each time my mother says
when you have kids, you'll understand the depth of my love for you.

as my abdomen begs
to time travel,
i learn that i no longer have one death to mourn,
but two:

      the love i have for the child i will never carry, and the love
      motherhood created for me.

i'll brake for a crow but won't slow for the edge

some things are destined to happen, and the rest can be yours if you chase
fate far enough.
i am sixteen,
       seventeen,
           eighteen,
convincing my journal that the ending of pain lives at the bottom of a
pill bottle.
and no one can convince me that i didn't want to die just because i
wanted to live too.
why else would i
dance in the rain with   razors in my pocket and laugh
under the sun   in long sleeves and jeans and squeeze
four friends into my bed, forgetting the mixed bag of
lexapro & tylenol severe taped behind my headboard?

no, i'm not suicidal, i just need out of me.
i can't include myself when i say *i'm so glad you're here*
to the friends who choose to hold me, and
i am the least safe when i am left alone
and when i am driving and see a family of crows eating trash in the
middle of the street.
i need to admit that i know they will see me coming
       and there is no good way to justify pulling the wheel towards
the ditch.
well, there is, if you care more about the potential
of hurting something else
than the act of hurting yourself.
there is, if you call it fate,

if you say you're destined to be alive   only because you haven't
died yet,
if you see that there is a world in which you could've kept driving
and the crows would have scattered
                and that sometimes
                    the better choice is not the one
we are begging to make.

the gravity of an outstretched hand

i need to tell you something.

> nothing weighs me down more than a heavy tongue,
> and it has pinned me to the bottom of the end of the earth.
> only skeletons live here,
> every version of me that has died
> while waiting to get better.
> my death feels more familiar than my mother's face.

i don't know how i can keep living this way.

i promise, i was over this

sometimes it gets so bad that i swear i have a stomach full of knots.
my entire life consists of untangling the grief inside me,
and i don't feel i have the strength to keep sifting through
the parts that hurt.

it's been bad for a while now, i just haven't said it.
the world is gentler to me when i pretend to love it back.
if i was honest about how much i thought about leaving,
it would open the ground beneath me, and
i won't let anyone fall because of me.

when i say it's getting bad,
i am not crying for help.
i am asking for mercy.
to live with sadness is to die each day.
i have lost every version of myself that i have ever loved,
and my insides have scratch marks from digging for what was left.
i really thought it wouldn't come back.

my hands are tired from a lifetime of undoing yesterday's knots.

please promise it won't always hurt to loosen the ties that made me

memory in passing

and here, you can see:
- a lifelike rendering of a dying girl,
- a silhouette of her mother,
- and a cell phone.

they are in the living room of their sixth family home, the one on the corner of lancaster and bristol. the creator of this moment is, in fact, the girl herself. not god or her parents, who believe themselves to be gods. to exist in a moment like this is proof that there has never been anyone watching over her. if you listen closely, you can hear a faint *why?* coming from the receiver. the artist has previously described this voice as her father's. she says he is there, in that moment, but not really. he was never there, for any moments, not really. he sounds frustrated because it is 3 p.m. on a wednesday and he is working. he can't leave the office even though his daughter is dying, and her mother is busy trying not to fade into the old photo on the wall where she is holding the girl and the girl is a child and very much alive.

now, please turn to the mother. it's clear her shadow is a metaphor for pain. there aren't many other things in life that will always follow you and grip your sneakers when you try to run towards the sun.

and then, there's the girl. her sleeves are rolled up and—please, she doesn't like when people look at her arms. it's horrible, really, this scene. they say life's short, but sometimes i think you can smell death from the second you take your first breath. anything that's ever been beautiful is just another ending. the girl knew this. she always knew this.

the artist left a note with this exhibit, and she would like me to read it to you:

"when the heart knows nothing but pain, you have already died. every other part of your body will follow. your legs will give. your lungs will seize. your mind will say there is no reason left to live if there is nothing left to feel. i was never someone worth remembering. so i made this scene for all of you, to leave a story you will never forget."

habitual

i wash my face / number my pores in a foggy mirror / paint my eyeliner / take it off / redo / take it off / redo / take it off / i have never been good at making things better / i am only good at quitting when it becomes a burden / i search for a shirt / *not that one* / the one with the longest sleeves and thinnest cloth / will myself to put it on / hide my hands / stretch the seams past my waist / when did everything become about disappearing / i find my jeans / remember that everyone does this the same way / one step at a time / i check my commute / *if you leave now, it'll take 20 minutes to arrive* / i don't know how living became a routine / breathing is only a reflex because we are too afraid of what happens when we quit / and yet / when the sun calls the moon / at the end of the day / i am always ready / unafraid / and wanting / to / end it

suicide in 9 ways

1. i taped a sandwich bag full of pills labeled "backup plan" behind the headboard of my childhood bed.

2. i left. like, really left. i drove 500 miles away because i can't love anything until i run from it.

3. i walked to the bridge every single day. i closed my eyes and pretended the world was flooding around me so i wouldn't have to jump.

4. i gave the rest of myself away. or he took it. or whatever hurts less to say.

5. i learned rock bottom was the feeling of the pavement after last call. i left my insides scattered throughout the city.

6. i fell in love.

7. i called the hotline on my lunch break. i said i couldn't keep going and he asked me how i wanted to do it. i told him i had the razors and he asked how i thought it would feel. *i don't know, probably great, randy.* he said i had no empathy when i talked about it, and *i don't. why would i? what's the point? why did i call?*

8. i went to treatment.

9. i kill myself every thursday at 9 a.m., when i tell my therapist it's hard for me to breathe. i kill myself every night at 10 p.m. with a handful of pills, but only the prescribed ones. i kill myself when i say *i love you* and when i kiss and hug and cry, and one day, i hope, there won't be any more sad parts of me to kill off.

spf

i've never known happiness as a friend,
only as a lover that melts my heart and leaves a mess of me in the dark.
it comes back.
anything that hurts always does.
i want happiness as much as i'm afraid of it.
hope illuminates, and
i don't want to swallow anyone with my light.
it's so much kinder to hold someone beneath the overcast.
there must be a place between the bottom of the universe and
the core of the sun, but i can't seem to find my way
out of the void i'm in right now.
i'm stuck protecting myself from the burn,
running for the shadows.

loving this life means understanding
the balance between
living   and fading into what's left.

the most beautiful ending

the greatest undoing happened when i took scissors
to the tourniquet you tied around my veins.
be still my heart,
for i have learned that bleeding out
would be a better death
than asphyxiating on your apologies.
i knew i'd die without you,
but no one told me how freeing being a
ghost would be.
i've visited all of the past versions of myself,
watched how love unraveled me onto the carpet,
endured when muddy men kept their dirty shoes on.

it's never too late to care for an open sore
or tend a healed wound.
realizing my worth was a resurrection.
i'd die
and die again
to be reborn into a heart that bleeds only
for me.

step 4
unfold

voice lessons

a schoolteacher once said
to be good, you must be
quiet.
i take my tongue and shove it so far down my throat that
i choke
on every hello.
swallow every goodbye.

i have grown to accept that
i am not good unless i am
holding back.

i want to swell my cries
until the birds sing for me
and we surround the earth
and everyone hears—

the wind will carry my lungs into the sky,
and i won't be silent
a day longer.

yearn

it's the lingering brush of the hand,
the exhale on the lips before a kiss,
the wind pulling the clouds from where you are
to me.

happiness is a loud, tender heaviness, and
loving you is the quiet
in between.

let's just say i'm definitely going to write a poem about it

because kissing her ruined me.
yes, i'm serious, it ruined me, since
yearning is just surviving the fear-triggered earthquake
that sparks the distance between
the head and the heart—

okay, she didn't ruin me,
but i want her to.
we're the strongest when we're tender enough
to feel the heaviness of doubt,
so no, i won't fight the crush—

i'll brace for impact.
tell myself *this could be nothing, but at least i am
honest about it this time.*
i'll write this silly poem.

i'll tell the whole world.

the one where no one leaves

today i was held and still wanted to walk away.
actually, i wanted to run.
sprint through the city so everyone would remember me as the person
they left behind.
climb to the edge
of the brooklyn bridge.
ask god why
i needed to be the one to take the fall.
jump just to leave an impact.

but i didn't leave.
today i let them cry when they said they loved me,
and i wept and promised a next time.
vowed a tomorrow of candy-covered teeth
and firefly tummies
and dancing in our underwear to one direction.
i said we could pretend to be thirteen again,
calling each other after 9 p.m. when the sky was quiet.
letting our laughter be the sun's alarm clock.

i think this means i'm getting better,
and i don't know if i want to.
i tell them i have already dug my grave
and it's waiting for me. they say,
so are all the flowers you could grow from the dirt.

today i broke every window in the greenhouse that keeps me.
i'm giving myself more room to feel the sun.

IF I'M TRULY
SCARED TO LOSE
THE ONES I LOVE,
THEN I SHOULD
FIGHT LIKE HELL
TO KEEP FROM
LOSING MYSELF

happy hour

she sips her gin and pineapple juice, and i watch
the week fall off her shoulders. the locals say
the seattle sun
is gone for the winter,
and i say they're fucking liars. because it's here;
i'm looking at it.
it's not cliché if i'm right. she is a girl
drinking with me at the bar
and she is also the light. and here i am, basking.
here i am,

                warm.

26

time has left me equidistant from
fourteen years old, sneaking
to the hastings by the high school to hide
the FIFTY SEX SECRETS edition of *cosmo*
inside *time*'s issue on
              THE FIRST BLACK PRESIDENT—
and from forty years old, where i imagine
i will swipe through the icloud archives to find
what's left of my youth.

i am not yet middle-aged,
but i'm somewhere
between hungry and brimming.
i'm still sad
because i don't know how to be
anything else.
i'm the most me i have ever been,
and i still don't know myself at all.

i will forever be
pulling from what was and
what could never be.

i need the tow of time to lead me
to the version of myself
who loves all the moments
she lived.

i shouldn't have watched that boeing plane-crash documentary before my flight

let's say the plane goes down.

let's say you can't hear me scream "i love you" because
it's hard to listen to each other
when we're afraid of what could happen next.
let's say the oxygen masks fall and i break the rules.
i help you with your mask before putting on mine because
fuck it, we're going down anyway.
the impact could be any second now,
and you say your life is rewinding in your head like an attic vhs.
i say "me too," except i'm lying.
what does it mean when something feels good to remember
but it wasn't good to live?
the world is about to end, so i don't want to
think about how we got here;
i'm choosing only to think about how we became.
how we met at that party and you said my name for the first time.
how in that moment i knew i wasn't invisible, *or maybe i am* and
loving me is your superpower.
you say you loved even the bad parts of us,
and i know it's real because we have nothing left to lose.
there's no stopping the spiral yet somehow i feel like i've already been
saved.
yes, i had a life before you, but with you   i have forever.

listen, i don't want this plane to nose-dive.
it's just hard for me to admit when i have something i'm afraid to lose,

because i don't want to be the reason it's gone.

so let's say we land in london and you kiss me when the wheels hit the
runway.
let's say we're *that couple* in the airport who makes everyone sick.
let's say we never go anywhere the other is not.
let's make our love the parachute.   the grass.   the sky.

i want to be a home full of memories of the way we love each other.
let's just, please,   always promise to survive
the falls.

welcome to the building

jenny in the condo next door somehow already knows our names.

she delivers a fingerprint-smeared tupperware
filled with curdled lemon bars
and shakes our hands like we're not still in the middle
of a goddamn pandemic.
the door shuts and i open the faucet to wash away jenny's palm sweat,
when my lover sneaks the sink hose and shoots at my heart.

i'm annoyed but i love him.
i love him and i'm soaked from tap water and lust
and he's laughing like a teen boy.

and i am finally a teen girl. *fuck off, jenny,*
there are no adults home.
we're busy baptizing our love in the dishwater
and tithing our shirts and hanes and socks
and eating the tortilla chip sacraments while
ass-naked on the counter.
i beg him to *eat me* on the counter.
we fuck on the barstools and
take a smoke break on the kitchen tile.

here, i am the afternoon sun puddle.
i am my younger self's fantasy
and it is better than my teenage dream;
it's real.
we are necking against the fridge while the magnets

fall onto us like fairy-tale rain.
i beg my lover to sing my name
and he brings the whole choir.
our love is too sacred to stay in these walls.
church is wherever we are, and i am not ashamed
if the whole city hears us
praising.
and i hope jenny never forgets the way it sounds
for us to come
home.

HOW BEAUTIFUL IT IS TO FINALLY SEE THAT I DESERVE TO BE LOVED SIMPLY BECAUSE I EXIST

season's feelings

christmas at 26 doesn't feel like christmas at all.

i wake up and eat a raw bagel and light the cinnamon candle.
i smoke a bowl and read mary oliver and cry, *really cry*, before noon.
i call my mom and dad and they say they miss me,
but i've never heard cheer so tired.
my partner rushes me to the patio
to kiss me under the first snowfall of winter. they say
see, the magic is still here.
i grieve and say
yes, but so is real life.
the memories are too, and the bad ones
love a holiday reunion.
most of living is remembering,
and i'm not ready to think about what hurts.
so i cope.
i yell
FUCK IT
to the clouds and run into the house and turn on every song that my
grandmother would say god hates. i serenade my partner with the help of
my invisible microphone and phoebe bridgers.
i cry, *really cry*, because they say they've never loved anyone more than
they love me
and i hate that.
i don't know how to feel love because i've spent so much of life
only knowing sorrow.
i'm living in a future i didn't plan for.
it is dazzling and delicate and terrible and ugly and *all, all mine.*

christmas at 26 doesn't feel like christmas at all.
but *look*. i am still here.
and jesus christ,

what a miracle.

the usual

i want the clichés with you. the guide-my-hands-and-show-me-how-to-strum-my-favorite-love-song for you. i want to forget my coat at your house, and i want you to run under the moonlight and climb through my window to return it. *we'll be a fairy tale, baby. kiss me until i wake up and you see the magic.* let me complain about the empty milk cartons in the fridge before we make out like teenagers against the cabinets. *i want you*, and maybe that makes you the cliché. maybe it means you'll choose the fear of loving me over the fear of losing me. maybe it means you'll stay when it's hard. maybe it means you'll love me. *please*, i really hope it means you'll   love me.

thursday-morning therapy session

i don't know if i'm happy or manic, but i got my nipples pierced last
night.
i was topless and alone with a stranger and the biggest fucking needle i've
ever seen.
i asked him to hurt me on purpose and i loved it. look at how beautiful \
pain can be
when i have the power to say when it ends.
maybe i'm manic. i want to bare my chest to anyone within arm's reach. \
look at me,
finally healing from this.
it might not be mania, but i don't want to be
happy. happiness leaves nothing to
blame the endings on.
if i'm happy, i have to admit
last night i got my nipples pierced because
i'm not afraid
of the things that hurt,
but it's true. i was happy yesterday and i was happy today and i don't \\
want to
think about tomorrow.

i just want to think about how hot i am naked.
how there's nothing to hide anymore.
how either way, it's beautiful to see this day,
when there is not one
bit of sadness.

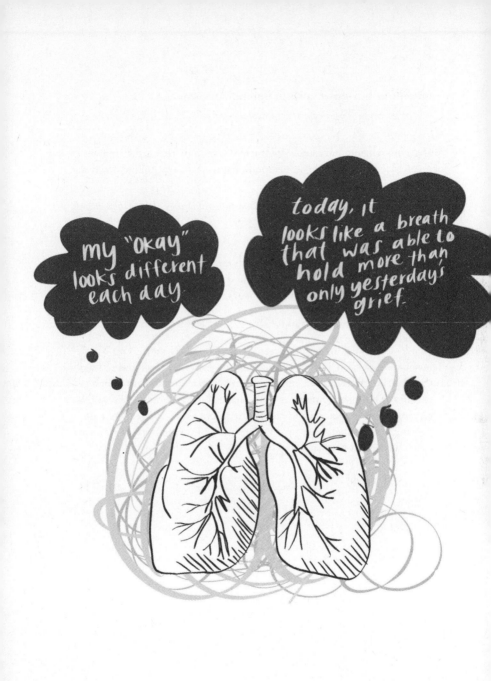

an ode to ball-gown girls in one-horse towns

after taylor swift & for the ones who cried to fearless (taylor's version)

i have no religion, but i know the ancient ceremony that is dancing with my shadow in my childhood bedroom. baptism is a tear rolling down my cheek while i sing

> *people are people and sometimes they change their minds.*

there is no scripture to explain the way love has unfolded me. i am not *fifteen* anymore, singing in my mirror about how i can only love boys with expiration dates. i am twenty-six and learning that i never truly learned how to let go when it's time. sure, love is painful but *wow,* so is becoming.

i am loving myself in a way my teenage self hoped i would. *it's fearless.* i may have grown up, but that didn't stop the yearning. i still love so loudly that the choir cannot drown my heartbeat. i am learning that the best part of the losing was finding myself in gospel. i am holy enough for this coming-of-age prayer. there is eternal life in my *forever and always.* i am dancing with my person in my living room, and crying because *i shine for him.* i have never been so full of light.

> so utterly and entirely filled with eternal life.

long-term relationship checklist as metaphors

or, there is a poem in everything we've built for this home

✓   the memories hanging by fridge magnets

✓   the sink spilling over beside an empty dishwasher

✓   the wedding photos on a dusty shelf

✓   the apology notes stuffed in junk drawers

✓   the alliterative footsteps in a stairwell homecoming

✓   the goodnight kisses in a chosen bed

✓   the cold feet and warm hands

✓   the loving

✓   the hurting

✓   the choice to trust the foundation,   every single day.

i wouldn't take it back but i would love to know how to get through it

stop caring.   about everything.

this feeling you have now is a terrible earworm,

and nothing matters more than the budding symphony inside your chest.

when your heartstrings start to tremble,

you'll learn that everything you use to quiet them will fail you.

make your throat sore from fighting against the words you'll want to

swallow down. if that gets too hard,

think about sophomore year,

       your face out the passenger-side window while josie went 85

down highway 6.

       remember how she said to scream every self-doubt into the

wind

       and how those beliefs have been swimming in the oklahoma air

ever since,

which reminds me,

don't go back.

you care about your hometown,

but you can't consider someplace home if you were lost the whole time

you were there.

and you won't find yourself anytime soon,

so don't try to look for yourself in someone else's bed,

       or the hardware store,

         or the bag of pills taped behind your bed.

i wish i could name the curse that is   growing up,

but all i can think of are synonyms of undoing.

stop yearning for someone else's love, and glow red for yourself.

adopt a cat and a dog, and don't be afraid to say yes when you mean it.

don't be afraid to mean it.
don't be afraid to live through this.
sweet girl, the best thing you can ever, ever do for yourself
is try.

wallflower

*i am both happy and sad at the same time, and i'm still trying to figure
out how that could be.*
—*stephen chbosky*, the perks of being a wallflower

when someone asks who i am,

my throat clenches,

remembering all the ways i have tried to

speak myself whole.

every night i am inconsolable, sitting in the grief of my yesterdays,

but in the morning, when the sun comes, i am singing with the radio.

i will line my stomach with pinch marks

but still dance to the music like i have never been made small.

i will stuff myself full with doubt but promise forever to anything i can

hold on to.

i am unsure of who i am outside of a dichotomy.

i am the crash point of sorrow and ecstasy.

i don't know how to be anything but everything.

and at the end of the day, i am learning

that i am becoming just who i am supposed to be.

nothing tears me open more than friendship

ari and keagan and amy and jesse could star in a film titled: forever.

ari and amy move to the midwest in 2007, and the local boys named keagan and jesse do not dare chase after a couple of renegades. these girls would fight to find their teenage dream, and while hindsight is clear and liberating, war is still war. they rage against the delusion that comes with growing up.

but there is no stopping time, and one day it is 2010 and the sixteen-year-old friends carpool home from the movies, out of breath in laughter while teasing jesse for necking isabelle during the end credits. ari and keagan and amy and jesse walk around the lake and climb rooftops. they smoke cigarettes in the backyard when the adults aren't home. they go to the antique store and search for anything that feels like yesterday did. they realize nothing ever will. they are there for each other as much as any teenager can be present for anything at all.

ari and keagan and amy and jesse go to school dances and take pictures and fall in love with each other in their parents' living rooms. they are the pioneers of becoming, as every high schooler is. they run after the sun and hold each other when it burns. they sneak into each other to try to fill the emptiness. they say things they don't mean. they rarely say the things they do mean.

by 2016, they are twenty-one. the only messages they send to each other are wedding invitations and funeral programs and breakups and breakdowns and *i love you*s and *forgive me*s and *living is getting to be too much*—so they talk about 2012. when they were both the cool kids and the misfits. crying in bathroom stalls and making out in the high school parking lot. ari was semi-formal queen and still tried to kill herself the night before prom. the movies don't show this part. imagine the critics at the premiere showing: four friends in ari's parents' house, tangled on the couch, watching a classic film. they laugh and cry, and then it ends. *everything fucking ends.* we can't be who we were forever, and that is the worst coming-of-age story there is. growing up looks like ari and keagan and jesse and amy sitting in their cars until midnight on a thursday. *are we going to make it out of this? can we please go back to where we started?*

ari and keagan and amy and jesse can't go back to 2007.

this is who we were and who i am. i'm now twenty-six, watching the highlight reel of adolescent ari and keagan and amy and jesse through the "on this day" memory tab on facebook. i don't know where i'm going, but i reminisce on the good ol' days to see frayed roots. it has taken everything in me to keep growing. to learn how to bloom anyway. i am a writer and not the doctor thirteen-year-old me swore i would be. i fell in and out of love with anyone who watered me, and i am still learning how to love myself first instead. i know where i come from and am being tender to the parts of me that were plucked and crushed and cloud-covered. i want to be me more than i don't want to be anything at all.

we can only wonder what thirteen-year-old ari would think about this. i wonder if she would know that one day, she and amy and keagan and jesse would be dancing at each other's weddings. i wonder if she would believe that even when the growing is hard,

there is always love to cling to.

i hated carly rae jepsen in high school just to feel edgy

the class of 2013 chose "*call me maybe*" to be our class song,
and i can't help but think we were foreshadowing.
we crossed the stage and cut every cord we knew with a tassel turn,
but no one told us we'd always be tethered to that goddamn place.
this is a poet's way of saying *i miss my friends.*
a manual on texting your old classmates: *call me, maybe, if you remember,*
a reading of our yearbook like the eulogy it was.
were these the good years,   or were we just alive?
we swore we were bulletproof, but we learned that joey and kaden and
seth and georgie weren't.
we thought we were invincible, but it only took one fucking needle to
bring jenny down.

> *call me, maybe, please, if you have time, if you want to talk*
> *about how most of us are just somebody's memory now.*

nine years ago we joked that we'd rather die before going to our ten-year
reunion,
and i fucking hate the kids that weren't joking about that. *call me,*
did you know sophia is pregnant? did you know charlie divorced their
husband?   *call me,*
and maybe this conversation will turn into our old lunch-hour gossip.
maybe we don't talk about our jobs and our partners and our new
depression medication and instead, we'll meet each other by our lockers
and start where we left off. *call me,*
and maybe we'll talk about the feeling of anticipation. we'll talk about
when *what if* was still *what if* and not   *what if i'm here now because i*
didn't then?   *call me, i miss you, and*
standing on the rooftop of the antique mall and smoking cigars and
tagging buildings and skipping class and being sad and passing notes and

dating a friend, and another, and another, and being really, really sad, and
running for gym,   towards insecurities,   away from the
mirages
our adolescent eyes could see,
because everything i thought i knew about the person i'd be is out of
sight now.
everything is different except for how it began.
maybe i'd go back, but only to remember the way it felt to want to be
someone.
i'd go back to corner myself before leaving that one-horse town just to
say,   *call them, not maybe,*
now, CALL THEM, apologize, CALL THEM, tell them how high school
is just how the grown-ups haze us to survive real life, CALL THEM,
NOW, I NEED YOU TO NOT BE AFRAID TO REMEMBER EVERY
MOMENT OF THIS.
it was the best fucking time of our lives.
and if it still aches, then maybe that means   it never really ended.

when bella says "where is the fucking moon?"

it doesn't matter where the moon is, i still trust the sky that holds her
on the nights the hunger for love returns.   why?
the moon is loyal and consistent and giving, and the stars, we are
what they became.
at dusk,
the light we see from the dippers and orion and the rest are just leftovers.
of course it's hard to sit in our feelings,   we're always
spinning,spinning,spinning trying to catch
                        up to the rest of the universe. it's no wonder humans
will start wars over yearning. we
        look up and we are looking at every yesterday.
the pain of desire never hits when you think it will, but we can be
prepared for anything
if we just ask for help. *it's okay to be someone who needs someone else.*
if i have to whisper those words to the sky before i can say them in the
mirror, then so be it.
i'll unfold under the moonlight until i, too, am full and new.

so look up.
the moon is right here, baby.
waxing and waning,
calling for tomorrow
as always.

you got a little closer
to your core.
that counts for something.

the ending of this story is not the ending of mine, or yours. discovering who you are will never be an easy unearthing. it can be the most painful thing you do.

thank you for being here as i unfold.

i hope it can help you, too.

acknowledgments

thank you, caitlin, for being the best editor, sounding board, and friend;
thank you, jessica and molly, for helping me fine-tune and
perfect this collection;
thank you, clara, kayla, and zane, for helping pull these poems out of me;
thank you, gerald, for supporting, holding, and celebrating me;
thank you, readers, for seeing and accepting me as a person and poet;

thank you, thank you, thank you.
i'm so happy you're here.

ari b. cofer (she/they) is a poet, writer, and the author of *paper girl and the knives that made her* and *unfold.* shortly after receiving her bachelor's degree in professional writing from baylor university, she, her husband, and their two pets relocated to the pacific northwest. ari's work has curated an engaged audience on social media and has been featured on sites such as buzzfeed.

while she enjoys a good love poem, she hopes to continue her mental health advocacy by writing on topics like depression, trauma, and recovery. visit her at aribcofer.com.